SOME MAJOR EVENTS IN WORLD WAR II

THE EUROPEAN THEATER

1939 SEPTEMBER—Germany invades Poland; Great Britain, France, Australia, & New Zealand declare war on Germany; Battle of the Atlantic begins. NOVEMBER—Russia invades Finland.

1940 APRIL—Germany invades Denmark & Norway. MAY—Germany invades Belgium, Luxembourg, & The Netherlands; British forces retreat to Dunkirk and escape to England. JUNE—Italy declares war on Britain & France; France surrenders to Germany. JULY—Battle of Britain begins. SEPTEMBER—Italy invades Egypt; Germany, Italy, & Japan form the Axis countries. OCTOBER—Italy invades Greece. NOVEMBER—Battle of Britain over. DECEMBER—Britain attacks Italy in North Africa.

1941 JANUARY—Allies take Tobruk. FEBRUARY—Rommel arrives at Tripoli. APRIL—Germany invades Greece & Yugoslavia. JUNE—Allies are in Syria; Germany invades Russia. JULY—Russia joins Allies. AUGUST—Germans capture Kiev. OCTOBER—Germany reaches Moscow. DECEMBER—Germans retreat from Moscow; Japan attacks Pearl Harbor; United States enters war against Axis nations.

1942 MAY—first British bomber attack on Cologne. JUNE—Germans take Tobruk. SEPTEMBER—Battle of Stalingrad begins. OCTOBER—Battle of El Alamein begins. NOVEMBER—Allies recapture Tobruk; Russians counterattack at Stalingrad.

1943 JANUARY—Allies take Tripoli. FEBRUARY—German troops at Stalingrad surrender. APRIL—revolt of Warsaw Ghetto Jews begins. MAY—German and Italian resistance in North Africa is over; their troops surrender in Tunisia; Warsaw Ghetto revolt is put down by Germany. JULY—allies invade Sicily; Mussolini put in prison. SEPTEMBER—Allies land in Italy; Italians surrender; Germans occupy Rome; Mussolini rescued by Germany. OCTOBER—Allies capture Naples; Italy declares war on Germany. NOVEMBER—Russians recapture Kiev.

1944 JANUARY—Allies land at Anzio. JUNE—Rome falls to Allies; Allies land in Normandy (D-Day). JULY—assassination attempt on Hitler fails. AUGUST—Allies land in southern France. SEPTEMBER—Brussels freed. OCTOBER—Athens liberated. DECEMBER—Battle of the Bulge.

1945 JANUARY—Russians free Warsaw. FEBRUARY—Dresden bombed. APRIL—Americans take B[elsen] and Buchenwald concentration camp[s]; Russians free Vienna; Russians take over Berl[in]; Mussolini killed; Hitler commits suicide. MAY—Ge[r]many surrenders; Goering captured.

THE PACIFIC THEATER

1940 SEPTEMBER—Japan joins Axis nations Ge[r]many & Italy.

1941 APRIL—Russia & Japan sign neutrality pa[ct]. DECEMBER—Japanese launch attacks against Pea[rl] Harbor, Hong Kong, the Philippines, & Mala[ya]; United States and Allied nations declare war on Ja[p]an; China declares war on Japan, Germany, & Ita[ly]; Japan takes over Guam, Wake Island, & Ho[ng] Kong; Japan attacks Burma.

1942 JANUARY—Japan takes over Manila; Jap[an] invades Dutch East Indies. FEBRUARY—Japan tak[es] over Singapore; Battle of the Java Sea. APRI[L]—Japanese overrun Bataan. MAY—Japan takes Ma[n]dalay; Allied forces in Philippines surrender to Ja[p]an; Japan takes Corregidor; Battle of the Coral Se[a]. JUNE—Battle of Midway; Japan occupies Aleutia[n] Islands. AUGUST—United States invades Guadalca[n]al in the Solomon Islands.

1943 FEBRUARY—Guadalcanal taken by U.[S.] Marines. MARCH—Japanese begin to retreat [in] China. APRIL—Yamamoto shot down by U.S. A[ir] Force. MAY—U.S. troops take Aleutian Islands ba[ck] from Japan. JUNE—Allied troops land in Ne[w] Guinea. NOVEMBER—U.S. Marines invade Bougai[n]ville & Tarawa.

1944 FEBRUARY—Truk liberated. JUNE—Saipan a[t]tacked by United States. JULY—battle for Gua[m] begins. OCTOBER—U.S. troops invade Philippine[s]; Battle of Leyte Gulf won by Allies.

1945 JANUARY—Luzon taken; Burma Road w[on] back. MARCH—Iwo Jima freed. APRIL—Okinawa a[t]tacked by U.S. troops; President Franklin Roosev[elt] dies; Harry S. Truman becomes presiden[t]. JUNE—United States takes Okinawa. A[U]GUST—atomic bomb dropped on Hiroshima; Russ[ia] declares war on Japan; atomic bomb dropped [on] Nagasaki. SEPTEMBER—Japan surrenders.

WORLD AT WAR

Road to Rome

WORLD AT WAR

Road To Rome

By R. Conrad Stein

Consultant:
Professor Robert L. Messer, Ph.D.
Department of History
University of Illinois, Chicago

 CHILDRENS PRESS ™

CHICAGO

British Prime Minister Winston Churchill felt that the
fastest and easiest way to bring World War II to an end would
be to defeat Italy and reach Germany from the south.

Library of Congress Cataloging in Publication Data

Stein, R. Conrad.
  The road to Rome.

  (World at war)
  Includes index.
  Summary: Discusses the Allied attempt to
remove the Axis powers from Italy in 1943, a
limited offensive carried out while preparations
were made for a giant invasion of France.
  1. World War, 1939–1945—Campaigns—
Italy—Juvenile literature. 2. Italy—History—
Allied occupation, 1943–1947—Juvenile
literature.
  [1. World War, 1939–1945—Campaigns—Italy.
2. Italy—History—Allied occupation,
1943–1947].
  I. Title. II. Series.
D763.I8S73 1983   940.54′21   82-17853
ISBN 0-516-04772-8

FRONTISPIECE:
American soldiers march past the Colosseum
in Rome on June 5, 1944, the day after the
city was taken.

PICTURE CREDITS:
UPI: Cover, pages 6, 8, 10, 17 (top left and
right, bottom left), 18, 20, 21, 23, 24, 31, 32,
33, 35, 36, 39, 42, 43, 45, 46
THE BETTMANN ARCHIVE: Pages 4, 27
U.S. ARMY PHOTOGRAPH: Page 9
WIDE WORLD: Pages 14, 28, 29
FPG: Pages 17 (bottom right), 40
HISTORICAL PICTURES SERVICE, CHICAGO:
Page 25
LEN MEENTS (Map): Page 13

COVER PHOTO:
An American soldier of the Fifth Army walks
through the rubble of the bomb-blasted and
shell-torn ruins of the town of Castleforte on
the road to Rome.

PROJECT EDITOR
Joan Downing

CREATIVE DIRECTOR
Margrit Fiddle

Salerno, Italy. Dawn. September 9, 1943. Some five hundred Allied ships pushed silently up to the beaches near this port city. Crowded into landing craft were thousands of tense soldiers. In a futile attempt to achieve surprise, warships in the American landing sector had been ordered not to fire. So, in the fading moonlight, the shores of Salerno looked like a picture on a postcard. But in the highlands stood German artillery pieces and tanks poised to turn the peaceful beaches into a nightmare of shellfire.

"The paramount task before us is . . . to strike at the soft underbelly of the Axis in effective strength, and in the shortest time." So wrote British Prime Minister Winston Churchill in November, 1942. Churchill believed the easiest path to Germany lay through Italy. Events in

On July 10, 1943, American troops landed in Sicily (above), and by
August 17, American, British, and Canadian forces had taken the island.

the weeks before the landing seemed to prove
him correct. In a successful campaign, the
British and American Allies had invaded and
taken the island of Sicily. It was a perfect
jumping-off place for an attack on Italy. The
crushing defeat in Sicily was almost the last
straw for the war-weary Italian people. They
rose up and deposed their dictator, Benito

On September 3, a few weeks after Mussolini's fall from power, Italy signed an armistice with the Allies. Above: United States General Dwight D. Eisenhower shakes hands with Lieutenant General Aldo Castillani, representative of the Italian government, after the signing.

Mussolini. Allied commanders hoped that meant Italy would fall without a fight. An American major wrote, "Speculation was we would dock in Naples with an olive branch in one hand and an opera ticket in the other." But after Mussolini's fall from power, Adolf Hitler rushed German divisions into Italy. The Italians, once partners of the Germans, suddenly became their captives.

A barrage of German artillery from the highlands (above) swept down
on American fighting men landing on the beaches of Salerno (below).

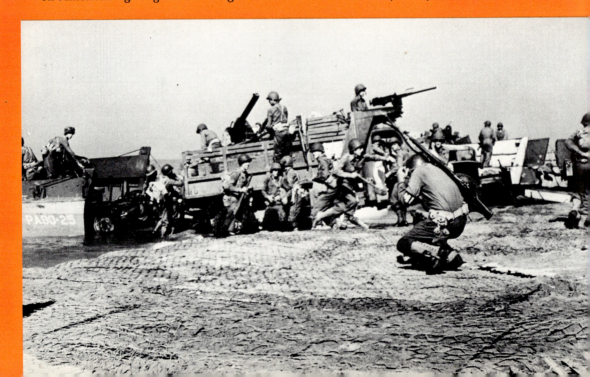

On the beaches of Salerno, the Allied troops found themselves in danger of being blasted into the sea. From the highlands, deadly German artillery swept the men crowded on the five-mile-wide beachhead. After a barrage that lasted for hours, the Germans set up loudspeakers near the Allied positions. In between bursts of shellfire, an English voice with a German accent announced, "Surrender, you Americans and Englishmen. You have no chance."

In the teeth of whistling shells and thundering explosions, Allied soldiers inched their way over the sand and rocks. Suffering horrible losses, they fought and crawled off the beach. The Germans counterattacked with tanks. The sands of the once peaceful, silvery beach flowed red. The battle for Salerno lasted nine days, and cost the Americans alone some 3,500 casualties. But finally the bloody beachhead was secured.

Almost two hundred miles to the north of Salerno, over a route of twisting, tortuous roads, lay the city of Rome. On this road to Rome the Allies encountered some of the most grinding, heartbreaking fighting of the war. Sadly, they discovered that Italy was not the "soft underbelly" of Europe that Churchill had predicted it would be.

To picture northern Italy, one could crush up a piece of paper, roll it into a cigar shape, and then crush it several times again. Italy is a long stem of land with towering mountain ranges that run its width and length. For military maneuvers, this type of terrain is a hell for the attacker, a paradise for the defender. A company of two hundred men dug in on high ground overlooking a road or valley can stop a battalion of a thousand men. A few well-placed troops can turn a mountain into a fortress.

SWITZERLAND

AUSTRIA

HUNGARY

Bolzano

Trento

Udine

Trieste

Como

Bergamo

Verona

Venice

YUGOSLAVIA

Turin

Milan

Po River

ALLIED INVASION
OF ITALY

Modera

Genoa

Bologna

Rimini

La Spezia

Florence

Ancona

Pisa

Ligurian Sea

Leghorn
(Livorno)

ITALY

Assisi

Adriatic Sea

Teramo

CORSICA

Rome

Ortona

GUSTAV LINE

Cassino

Termoli

Faggia

Anzio

Formia

Bari

Sessa Aurunca

Naples

Brindisi

Pompeii

Salerno

Capri

Taranto

SARDINIA

Tyrrhenian Sea

Crotone

Pizzo

Mediterranean Sea

Trapani

Palermo

Messina

Reggio di Calabria

Marsala

SICILY

Catania

Niscemi

Licata

Gela

Ragusa

Tunis

TUNISIA

A

Field Marshal
"Smiling Albert"
Kesselring
commanded the
German forces
in Italy.

Commanding the German forces was a superb field marshal named Albert Kesselring. His press photos showed him with a perpetual grin, and Allied soldiers nicknamed him "Smiling Albert." Privately, Kesselring hated German dictator Adolf Hitler. But he was an old soldier who believed in obeying his superiors. His orders read: "The *Führer* [leader] expects the bitterest struggle for every yard." Kesselring had a keen eye for making mountains and river valleys work for him. He knew that in a defensive war, land could be more important than firepower.

In the mountains about a hundred miles south of Rome, Kesselring himself supervised the construction of what was called the Gustav Line. This was a formidable defensive barrier that stretched across the stem of Italy. It was so strong that Kesselring predicted that the "British and Americans will break their teeth on it."

The German field marshal insisted that his men dig foxholes and trenches on ground so steep that the Allies would practically have to crawl on all fours just to get within rifle range. He stationed artillery spotters on dizzying mountain peaks where they could see for miles. He ordered his troops to build machine-gun nests encased in steel and reinforced concrete. And in front of these positions Kesselring had his men string barbed wire and plant land mines.

After fighting their way north from Salerno, the Allies marched directly into this awesome maze of defenses. The road to Rome turned into a bloodbath. The soldiers in the highly fortified German positions had only to wait for Allied troops to attack, and then cut them down. The Gustav Line was not only strong, it was also deep. Even if the Germans were forced to retreat a few hundred yards, they simply moved into the next well-prepared position. The Allies discovered that behind every mountain in Italy there was always another mountain. And it seemed that Field Marshal Kesselring had machine guns, barbed wire, and land mines on every one of them.

In chess, a stalemate occurs when the game reaches a point where neither player can win. In front of the Gustav Line, a long, ugly stalemate began. The Allies could not move forward. The Germans refused to pull back. Yet the fighting raged on.

Above: Allied troops fighting in the mountains of Italy had to
deal with the awesome defenses of Kesselring's Gustav Line, which
included machine-gun nests, barbed wire, and deadly land mines.
Below: The first Allied troops to enter the bomb-scarred ruins of
Naples three weeks after the Salerno landings were given a joyful welcome.

The fighting in Italy's rugged mountains became a grinding, inch-by-inch ordeal.

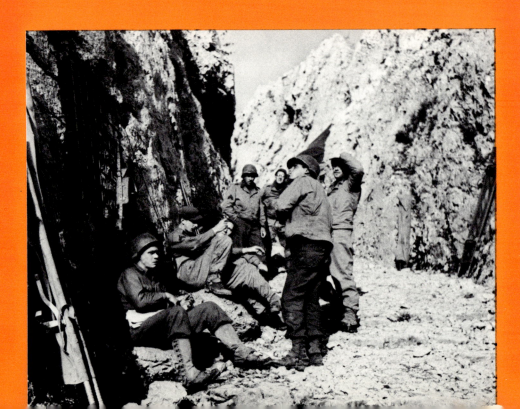

The war in Italy was further complicated by disagreements in the Allied high command. American generals considered Italy to be a sideshow and wanted to concentrate Allied efforts on the coming invasion of France. British strategists, led by Churchill, believed that the Allied forces could sweep through Italy and invade Germany from the south. Because of Allied bickering, the Italian campaign lacked a cohesive plan. The battles grew in intensity, but the war in Italy had no clear aim.

In Italy's rugged mountains, the fighting became a grinding, inch-by-inch ordeal. The mountains made mass movement of troops impossible. Ground fighting was carried out by patrols of only twenty to thirty men. War correspondent Eric Sevareid described this patrol action as "slow, spasmodic movement from one patch of silence to another."

American troops piled sandbags to build a protective wall around a first-aid station nestled into the side of a craggy mountain.

Allied superiority in tanks and trucks meant almost nothing. Army vehicles were unable to roll over the steep, twisting mountain roads. A mule became more valuable than a fleet of trucks. Ironically, ten years earlier a splendid mule corps had been assigned to the American army's cavalry units. Then the army became mechanized and the mule corps was discontinued. Now machines were nearly useless and army commanders longed to see their old mules once more.

he constant, drenching winter rains turned the Italian front into a sea of mud.

The winter brought northern Italy drenching rain during the day and bone-chilling cold at night. On both sides, pneumonia brought down more men than did bullets. The men lived in foxholes that had walls made of mud at noon and ice at midnight. Every day the Allied troops crawled out of their holes to go on patrols seeking weak points in the German lines. But there were no weak points. Kesselring had made sure of that.

Although the Americans lived a cruel routine of mud, misery, and battle, several writers and artists still tried to capture their life-style for the families back home. Two of those men became famous.

A small, gray-haired newspaper writer from Indiana named Ernie Pyle traveled from unit to unit in Italy. Pyle spent little time with the generals who slept in comfortable beds miles away from the fighting. He preferred to live with and write about the foot-slogging GIs who suffered at the front. Pyle wrote, "Our troops were living in almost inconceivable misery. The fertile black valleys were knee-deep in mud. Thousands of men had not been dry for weeks. Other thousands lay at night in high mountains with the temperatures below freezing and the thin snow sifting over them. They dug into the stones and slept in little chasms and behind rocks in half-caves. How they survived the dreadful winter at all was beyond us. . . ."

The everpresent mud slowed down men and vehicles alike. Above: Two Italians scrape some of the gooey mud from the uniform of a British sergeant.
Below: U.S. Army engineers tackle the problem of repairing a flooded bypass.

Though the field soldiers pictured below had to use hay to provide dry beds in their muddy-floored tents, a few, including the men of the Fifth Army pictured above, were able to utilize old mountain caves for protection against German shelling.

Among the unorthodox weapons used by the Germans in Italy were concrete "bowling balls" (left) that were rolled downhill toward advancing Allied troops. Cartoonist Bill Mauldin (right) created Willie and Joe, two unshaven, weary-looking American foot soldiers in Italy (opposite page).

Pyle described the savage combat along the Gustav Line this way: "The fighting on the mountaintop reached the caveman stage sometimes. Americans and Germans were frequently so close that they actually threw rocks at each other. Many more hand grenades were used than in any other phase of the Mediterranean war. And you have to be pretty close when you throw hand grenades."

Another American portrayed the life of foot soldiers in Italy by drawing cartoons. Sergeant Bill Mauldin had studied cartooning only through a course he took by mail. Yet he created

"Let 'im in. I wanna see a
critter I kin feel sorry fer."

"I need a couple guys what don't owe me
no money fer a little routine patrol."

two unforgettable cartoon characters called
Willie and Joe. Willie and Joe were always
pictured as two unshaven, weary-looking soldiers
who wore baggy uniforms. Mauldin's cartoons
appeared in GI newspapers and in newspapers
in the United States. In his book *Up Front*,
Mauldin said, "I'm a cartoonist; maybe I can be
funny after the war, but nobody who has seen
this war can be cute about it while it's going on.
The only way I can try to be a little funny is to
make something out of the humorous situations
which come up even when you don't think life
could be any more miserable."

At the heart of the Gustav Line towered the seventeen-hundred-foot Monte Cassino. That mountain, more than any other, symbolized the frustration felt by the Allies during the Italian campaign.

Monte Cassino blocked the way to a long, narrow valley that led straight to Rome. There was no way around the mountain. The Allies had to take it. But German artillery spotters who were dug in on the mountain's peak directed a storm of shellfire on any Allied soldier bold enough to stick his head out of his foxhole. The Allied troops believed that German artillery spotters were hiding in a marvelous old monastery perched on the top of Monte Cassino.

Waging war in any part of Italy was like waging war in a museum. War destroys more than lives. Shells and bombs have no respect for historic buildings or magnificent works of art. Already the war in Italy had destroyed buildings that dated back to Roman times. The monastery

The Benedictine monastery on Monte Cassino (skyline) was
untouched before the February 15, 1944 Allied bombing attack.

at Monte Cassino was one of the most important
Catholic shrines in the world. Because of its
religious and artistic importance, the Allied
commanders were reluctant to bomb it. But
weeks dragged by and many lives were lost.
Finally the command was given and American
bombers dropped six thousand tons of high
explosives on the ancient monastery. In one
morning, a building that had stood for centuries
was utterly destroyed.

Though six thousand tons of high explosives had reduced the monastery to a pile of rubble, Allied forces were unable to take the hill. Ironically, the ruins gave the Germans superb protection from which to launch their attacks.

After the war it was discovered that the venerable monastery had held not a single German soldier. The German commander at Monte Cassino was General Fridolin von Senger, a devout Catholic. Von Senger refused to station his men anywhere near the monastery because he did not want the building to be a target for bombs and shells. The German general had even posted guards near the building so no stray German soldier could loot the artworks. All that the bombing accomplished was to kill about three hundred village people and several Benedictine monks who were inside the monastery praying. The Allies had dropped leaflets announcing that the building would be bombed. Still, many people chose to stay inside, believing that the religious shrine was too important to be destroyed.

After the bombing, General von Senger allowed his men to dig positions in the rubble of the ancient building. If anything, the air raid on the monastery strengthened the German hold on Monte Cassino.

Because of the stalemate on the front, Allied commanders began planning what they called an "end run." At sea, the Allies had complete command. They began to plan an amphibious landing behind German lines. Such a landing would force Kesselring to take some of his troops off the Gustav Line. Then the Allies could break through the Gustav Line and link up with the landing party. Winston Churchill favored such a landing. He was still convinced that the best way to Germany was through the Mediterranean. Churchill endorsed an Allied plan to land two divisions at a town called Anzio, thirty-three miles south of Rome.

American General John P. Lucas
was in charge of the Anzio landings.

The initial landing went well. "We achieved
what is certainly one of the most complete
surprises in history," wrote American General
John P. Lucas, who was in charge of the
operation. By the end of the first day, the Allies
had 36,000 men and more than 3,000 tanks,
trucks, and jeeps on the beach. But crafty Field
Marshal Kesselring had long expected the Allies
to land troops somewhere to his rear. He had
kept strategic reserves in the north of Italy to
counter any such landings. Now he rushed those
reserves to Anzio.

At Anzio, the Allies took an extraordinarily
long time to start their march north toward
Rome. General Lucas, a cautious man, wanted
to have a huge stockpile of supplies on the beach
before he began his advance. Instead of moving
forward, he kept his men busy unloading ships.

German attacks on the Anzio landing forces (right)
kept the Allies pinned down on the beachhead (left).

Kesselring's divisions got to Anzio before the
men there could start their offensive.

Anzio quickly became a disaster for the Allies.
Powerful German counterattacks forced the
landing party to retreat to their beachhead. With
their backs to the sea, the Allies dug trenches
and strung barbed wire to try to stop the
onrushing Germans. The Anzio landing force
had been planned as a spearhead for the drive to
Rome. Now the attackers had become defenders
and were in danger of being thrown into the sea.

The beautiful homes lining the Nettuno waterfront adjoining Anzio
became targets for the Germans during their attacks on the Allies.

Left: War correspondents Ernie Pyle (left) and Sergeant George Aarons discuss their narrow escape from death during the German shelling of Anzio. Right: An American soldier from Brooklyn gives an old Italian woman wheelbarrow taxi service during her flight toward Allied lines at Anzio.

In London, Winston Churchill fumed about the desperate situation at Anzio. He blamed the failure on General Lucas's lack of aggression. About Anzio, Churchill wrote, "I had hoped that we were hurling a wildcat onto the shore, but all we got was a wounded whale."

According to plans, the Anzio landing was to be combined with an Allied breakout in the south. But the Allies could not budge the stubborn Germans from their positions on the

Gustav Line. Allied attacks were driven back by hellish rains of shellfire. Many of the guns that fired at the Allied troops were the famous and feared 88s. The German 88-mm triple-purpose gun could be used as an antitank gun, an antiaircraft gun, or an artillery piece. The gun had a long range and an uncanny accuracy.

The German gunners were experts. In fact, most of the troops who fought for Kesselring were the toughest and most experienced soldiers in the German army. "Whatever we may feel about the Germans," said British General Harold Alexander, "we must admit that German soldiers [in Italy] were extremely tough and brave."

As the war in Italy dragged on, the Allied troops there became forgotten soldiers. People at home wanted to read newspaper stories telling of glorious victories or bold offensives. Few people cared to read about men locked in a bloody struggle that seemed to be going nowhere.

Above: A group of Italian children watch a British Eighth Army Sherman tank as it rumbles its way past them.
Below: All along the road to Rome, shattered Italian towns attested to the destruction of war.

As American and British units were pulled out of Italy to take part
in preparations for the D-Day landings at Normandy, France, international
troops were shipped in to take their places. These troops of the
Brazilian Expeditionary Forces were camped in a staging area near Pisa.

Even the Allied commanders seemed to forget
about the Italian front. They were busy
preparing for the massive invasion of France.
One by one, American and British units were
pulled out of Italy and sent to England to train
for that invasion. The Allied forces in Italy
became more and more international. Troops
from Poland, France, Brazil, India, Morocco,
and Algeria were shipped there. By early 1944,
fewer than one third of the Allied troops on the
Italian front were American.

Throughout the winter of 1943-44, the bloody stalemate continued. The Gustav Line seemed impregnable. The Allied "spearhead" at Anzio had been reduced to a huddled bunch of surrounded troops. And Monte Cassino, with a wrecked monastery on its crest, remained solidly in German hands.

But by spring, the stagnant front was alive with movement. American and British troops fought their way across the Rapido River. That river had been the scene of much bloody combat. Algerian soldiers, many of whom lived in the mountains of North Africa, advanced over the rugged mountain chain west of Cassino. These mountain warriors made the first dent in the Gustav Line. And at Cassino the Allies dragged more than sixteen hundred heavy guns up to a twenty-five-mile front. On May 11, artillery officers shouted a one-word command: "Fire!"

The earth trembled. Monte Cassino seemed to disappear under a thick cloud of smoke. When the smoke lifted, silent infantrymen slipped out of their foxholes and moved forward. Three previous major assaults on Monte Cassino had failed. The fourth assault would be carried out by a unit of dedicated Polish soldiers.

For the Poles, Italy was the end of a long and heartbreaking journey. They had been captured by the Russians when Germany and Russia divided Poland in 1939. They were released two years later when Germany invaded Russia. Then the Polish soldiers traveled south through Iran to link up with Allied forces in North Africa. Finally, the Allies shipped them to Italy. These Polish soldiers had traveled thousands of miles and waited five years for this battle. Many had lost their entire families during the war and felt they had little reason to go on living. German 88s blasted the Polish troops as they crawled up Monte Cassino. But they kept going. When they ran out of ammunition, the Poles threw rocks at

The destruction of Cassino (above) and the Benedictine
monastery on the hill overlooking the town was nearly complete before
Allied forces finally won the Battle of Cassino on May 18, 1944.

the Germans. After six days of furious combat,
the Polish flag fluttered above the ruins of the
monastery on top of the mountain. The battle
had cost some four thousand Polish lives.

Facing Allied advances everywhere, Kesselring
ordered a retreat from the Gustav Line. After
the German retreat, events moved quickly in
Italy. By May 22, French forces crossed the
river Liri. Three days later, the American Fifth
Army linked up with the landing party at Anzio.

On June 5, 1944, an enormous crowd of joyful Romans jammed St. Peter's Square (above) to give the Allied forces a wild, spontaneous welcome. One woman in the crowd (below) held a newspaper with the headline: "Days of exultation for Rome."

By June 2, the Germans declared Rome to be an open city—unoccupied and therefore not to be attacked.

After nine grueling months, the Allies had come to the end of the long and bloody road to Rome.

On June 5, 1944, the day after the Allied troops had entered the city, it seemed as if everyone in Rome poured out to greet the Allies. People cheered and waved wildly as the men marched through the winding streets of the ancient city. American General Mark Clark described the scene: "There were gay crowds in the streets, many of them waving flags, as our infantry marched through the capital. Flowers were stuck in the muzzles of the soldiers' rifles and in those of guns on the tanks. Many Romans seemed to be on the verge of hysteria in their enthusiasm for the American troops."

The Allied invasion of France on D-Day, June 6, 1944, only two days
after the liberation of Rome, opened the door to victory in Europe.

Finally, world attention had returned to the
"forgotten" soldiers in Italy. But the men did
not enjoy fame for very long. Two days after the
liberation of Rome, General Dwight D.
Eisenhower, Supreme Allied Commander in
Europe, launched the Allied invasion of France.
Once more, the headlines back home told news
of other, more exciting fronts.

American troops face the Victor Emmanuel II Memorial in Rome on July 4, 1944.

The fighting continued in Italy until the last month of the war. North of Rome, Kesselring continued his skilled defense. The massive breakthrough into Europe's so-called soft underbelly never occurred.

Military historians often write about great mistakes made by leaders during wartime. Some historians believe the entire Italian campaign was a mistake for the Allies. They say the Allies continued their long, tough fight in Italy only to please Churchill. Critics also say that if the Allies had concentrated their efforts on an invasion of France in 1943, the war in Europe could have ended at least a year earlier. But all that is guesswork. Certainly the Allied offensive in Italy kept twenty-six German divisions tied down. If they had not been fighting in Italy, those same men would have been fighting against the Russians, or fighting to repel an Allied invasion of northern Europe.

The battle for Italy might seem somewhat like a chess game to some students of World War II.

War correspondent
Ernie Pyle
lived with and
wrote about the
long-suffering
troops who
fought in Italy.

But suffering and death are no game. Ernie Pyle
wrote this about the death of an American
company commander somewhere on the Italian
front: "I was at the foot of the trail the night
they brought Captain Waskow down. The moon
was nearly full, and you could see far up the
trail. . . . Then a soldier came. . . and bent over,
and he too spoke to his dead captain, not in a
whisper but awfully tenderly, and he said, 'I
sure am sorry, sir.' "

Life went on for these Italian women, who kept right on scrubbing their clothes as bombs fell nearby at the Anzio beachhead.

Index

Page numbers in boldface type indicate illustrations.

About the Author

Mr. Stein was born and grew up in Chicago. At eighteen he enlisted in the Marine Corps where he served three years. He was a sergeant at discharge. He later received a B.A. in history from the University of Illinois and an M.F.A. from the University of Guanajuato in Mexico.

Although he served in the Marines, Mr. Stein believes that wars are a dreadful waste of human life. He agrees with a statement once uttered by Benjamin Franklin: "There never was a good war or a bad peace." But wars are all too much a part of human history. Mr. Stein hopes that some day there will be no more wars to write about.